TIMPANI

ENSEMBLE DEVELOPMENT

Chorales and Warm-up Exercises for Tone, Technique and Rhythm

INTERMEDIATE CONCERT BAND

Peter **BOONSHAFT** | Chris **BERNOTAS**

Thank you for making *Sound Innovations: Ensemble Development* a part of your concert band curriculum. With 412 exercises, including over 70 chorales by some of today's most renowned composers for concert band, it is our hope you will find this book to be a valuable resource in helping you grow in your understanding and abilities as an ensemble musician.

An assortment of exercises are grouped by key and presented in a variety of intermediate difficulty levels. Where possible, several exercises in the same category are provided to allow for variety while accomplishing the goals of that specific type of exercise. You will notice that many exercises and chorales are clearly marked with dynamics, articulations, style, and tempo for you to practice those aspects of performance. Other exercises are intentionally left for you or your teacher to determine how best to use them in reaching your performance goals.

Whether you are progressing through exercises to better your technical facility or to challenge your musicianship with beautiful chorales, we are confident you will be excited, motivated, and inspired by using *Sound Innovations: Ensemble Development*.

ISBN-10: 0-7390-8786-X
ISBN-13: 978-0-7390-8786-2

Instrument photos courtesy of Yamaha Corporation of America Band & Orchestral Division

Concert B♭ Major

1 **PASSING THE TONIC**

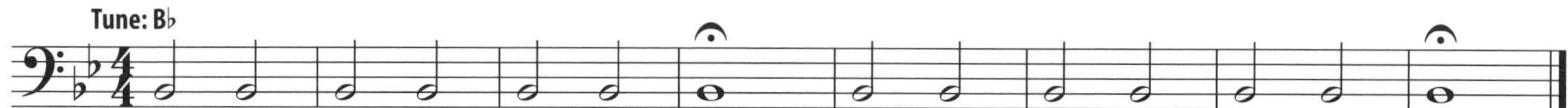

2 **PASSING THE TONIC**

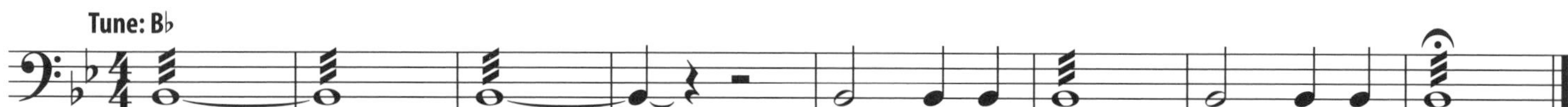

3 **PASSING THE TONIC**

4 **PASSING THE TONIC**

5 **PASSING THE TONIC**

6 **BREATHING AND LONG TONES**

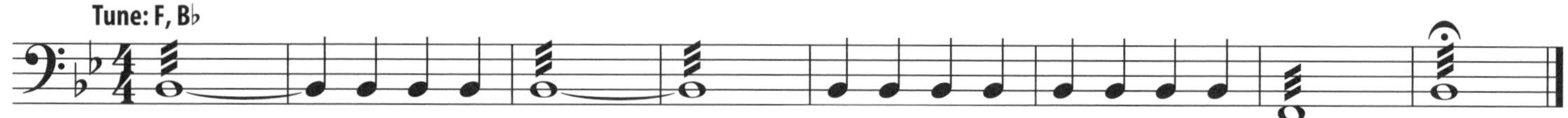

7 **BREATHING AND LONG TONES**

8 **BREATHING AND LONG TONES**

9 **BREATHING AND LONG TONES**

10 **CONCERT B♭ MAJOR SCALE**

11 **SCALE PATTERN**

12 **SCALE PATTERN**

13 **SCALE PATTERN**

14 **SCALE PATTERN**

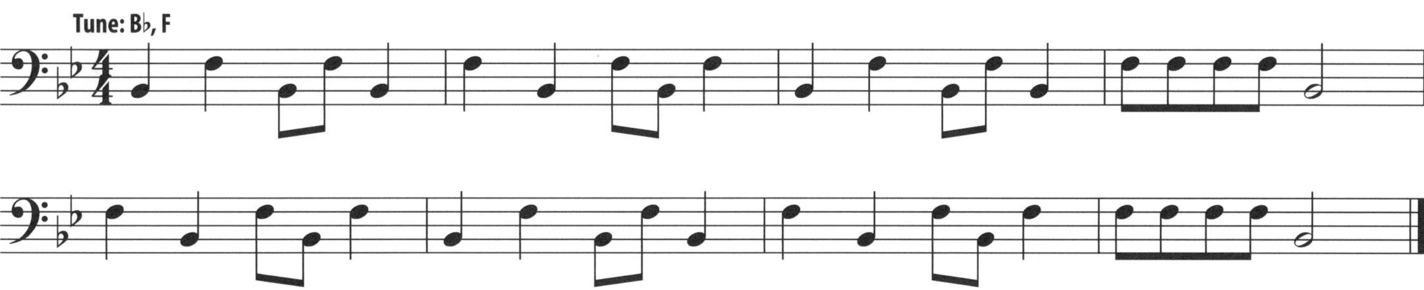

15 **SCALE PATTERN**

16 **CHANGING SCALE RHYTHM**

17 **CONCERT B♭ CHROMATIC SCALE**

18 **FLEXIBILITY**

Tune: F, B♭

19 **FLEXIBILITY**

Tune: F, B♭

20 **ARPEGGIOS**

Tune: F, B♭

21 **ARPEGGIOS**

Tune: F, B♭

22 **INTERVALS**

Tune: F, B♭

23 **INTERVALS**

Tune: B♭, F

24 **BALANCE AND INTONATION: PERFECT INTERVALS**

Tune: B♭

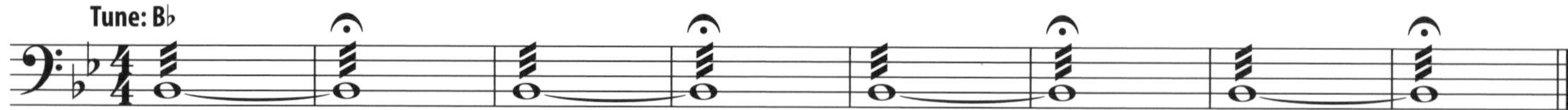

25 **BALANCE AND INTONATION: DIATONIC HARMONY**

Tune: F, B♭, E♭

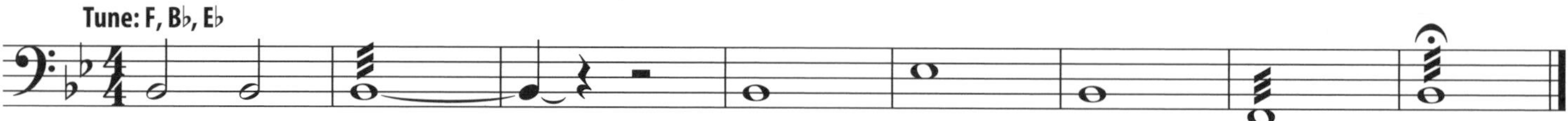

26 **BALANCE AND INTONATION: FAMILY BALANCE**

Tune: B♭

27 **BALANCE AND INTONATION: LAYERED TUNING**

Tune: B♭

28 **BALANCE AND INTONATION: MOVING CHORD TONES**

Tune: F, B♭

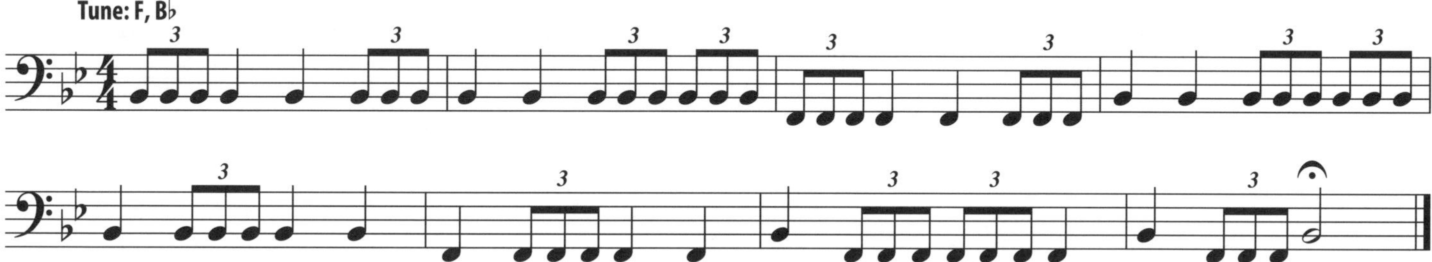

29 **BALANCE AND INTONATION: SHIFTING CHORD QUALITIES**

Tune: B♭

30 **EXPANDING INTERVALS: DOWNWARD IN PARALLEL OCTAVES**

Tune: B♭, F

31 **EXPANDING INTERVALS: DOWNWARD IN PARALLEL FIFTHS**

Tune: B♭, F

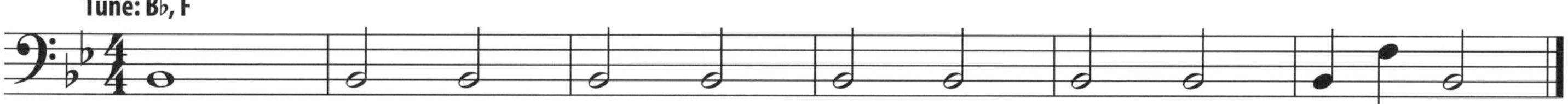

32 **EXPANDING INTERVALS: DOWNWARD IN TRIADS**

Tune: B♭, F

33 **EXPANDING INTERVALS: UPWARD IN PARALLEL OCTAVES**

Tune: B♭, E♭

34 **EXPANDING INTERVALS: UPWARD IN TRIADS**

Tune: B♭, E♭

35 **RHYTHM**

Tune: B♭

36 **RHYTHM**

37 **RHYTHM**

38 **RHYTHM**

39 **RHYTHM**

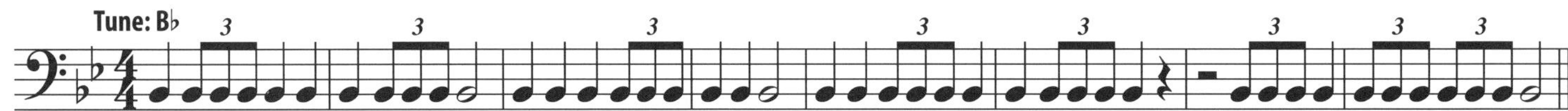

40 **RHYTHMIC SUBDIVISION**

41 **RHYTHMIC SUBDIVISION**

42 **RHYTHMIC SUBDIVISION**

43 **METER**

44 **PHRASING**

45 **PHRASING**

46 **ARTICULATION**

47 **DYNAMICS**

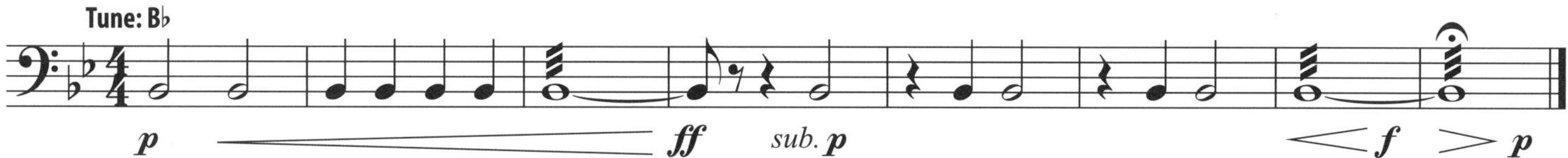

48 **ETUDE**

49 **ETUDE**

50
CHORALE: JESU, MEINE ZUVERSICHT
Johann Cruger (1598—1662)
Arranged by Todd Stalter
Adagio
Tune: F, B♭
5
2
mf
51
CHORALE
Michael Story (ASCAP)
Moderato
Tune: F, B♭
5
mf
rit.
52
CONCERT B♭ MAJOR SCALE & CHORALE
Chris M. Bernotas (ASCAP)
A
Tune: F, B♭
B
ff
53
CHORALE
Chris M. Bernotas (ASCAP)
Andante
Tune: F, B♭, E♭
5
mp
mf
rit.
mp
54
CHORALE
Randall D. Standridge (ASCAP)
Med. Soft Mallets
Tune: F, B♭
5
mf
9
13
f
mf
55
CHORALE
Andrew Boysen, Jr.
Moderately slow
Tune: F, B♭, G
8
10
A tempo
9
rit.
20
p
ff
p
fff
p
fff

56 CHORALE
Gently
Tune: B♭, E♭
cantabile
Ralph Ford (ASCAP)
5
p
mf
mp
p
molto rit.
57 CHORALE
Larghetto
Tune: B♭, E♭
Robert Sheldon
2
mf
2
11
f
mp poco rall.
58 CHORALE
Roland Barrett
Tune: F, B♭
5
4
p
mp
p
9
2
13
p
mp
p
17
4
21
p
mf
59 CHORALE
Tenderly
Tune: F, B♭, E♭
Chris M. Bernotas (ASCAP)
5
mp
f
9
13
mp
mf
rit.
60 CHORALE
Majestic
Medium Mallets
Tune: F, B♭, E♭
Rossano Galante
mf
7
2
f
11
mf
f
mf
f rit.

Concert G Minor

61 **PASSING THE TONIC**

62 **BREATHING AND LONG TONES**

63 **CONCERT G NATURAL MINOR SCALE**

64 **CONCERT G HARMONIC AND MELODIC MINOR SCALES**

65 **SCALE PATTERN**

66 **CONCERT G CHROMATIC SCALE**

67 **FLEXIBILITY**

68 **FLEXIBILITY**

69 **ARPEGGIOS**

70 **ARPEGGIOS**

71 **INTERVALS**

72 **INTERVALS**

73 **BALANCE AND INTONATION: DIATONIC HARMONY**

74 **BALANCE AND INTONATION: MOVING CHORD TONES**

75 **BALANCE AND INTONATION: LAYERED TUNING**

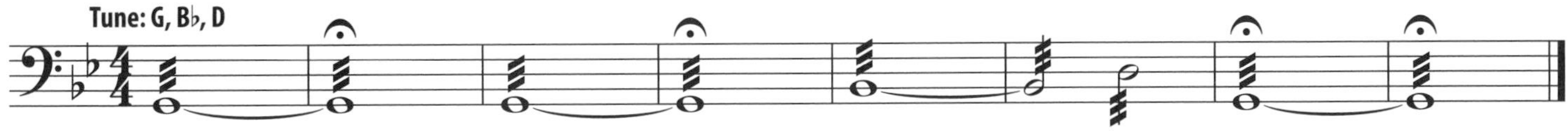

76 **BALANCE AND INTONATION: FAMILY BALANCE**

77 **EXPANDING INTERVALS: DOWNWARD IN PARALLEL FIFTHS**

78 **EXPANDING INTERVALS: UPWARD IN PARALLEL THIRDS**

79 **RHYTHM**

80 **RHYTHM**

81 **RHYTHM**

82 **RHYTHMIC SUBDIVISION**

83 **RHYTHMIC SUBDIVISION**

84 **ARTICULATION AND DYNAMICS**

85 **ETUDE**

86 **CHORALE**

Robert Sheldon

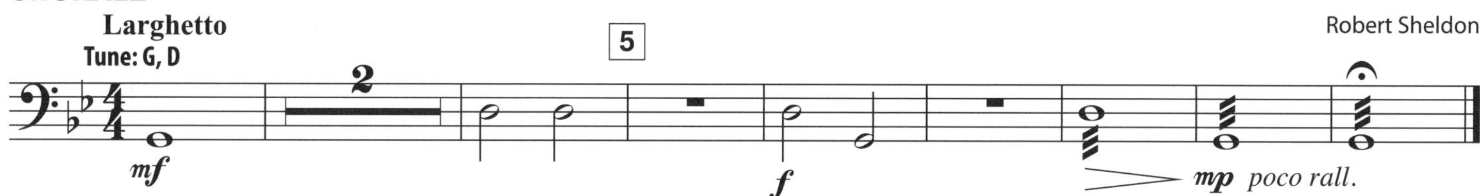

87 **CHORALE**

Michael Story (ASCAP)

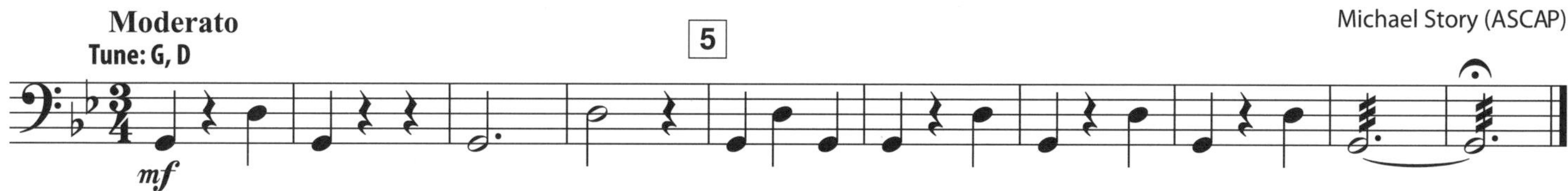

88 **CONCERT G MINOR SCALE & CHORALE**

Chris M. Bernotas (ASCAP)

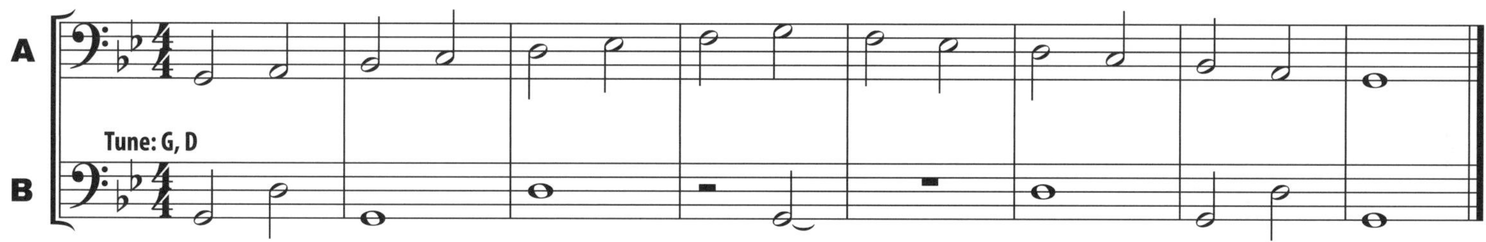

89 **CHORALE**

Andrew Boysen, Jr.

90 **CHORALE**

Rossano Galante

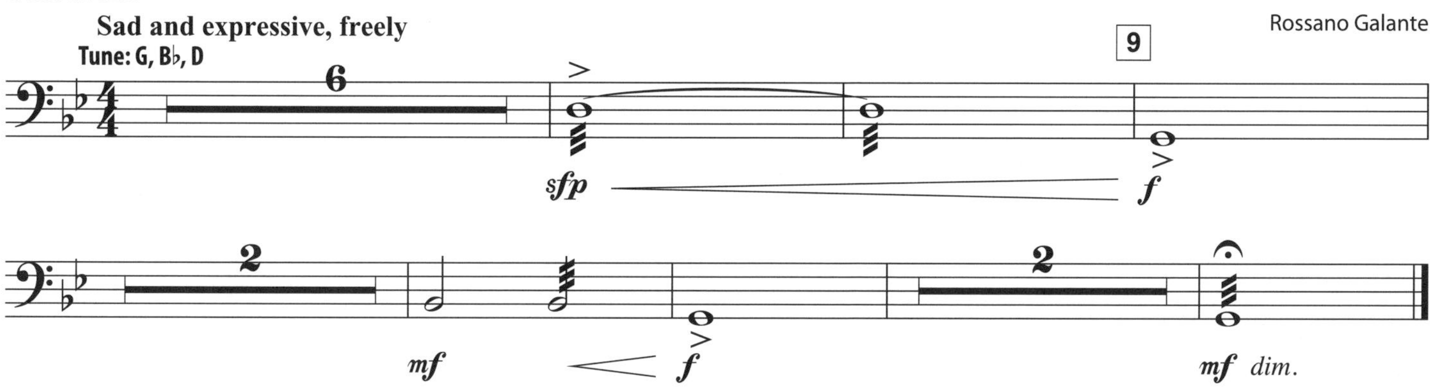

Concert E♭ Major

91 **PASSING THE TONIC**

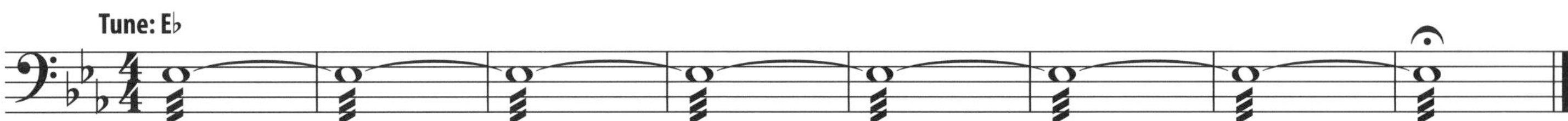

92 **PASSING THE TONIC**

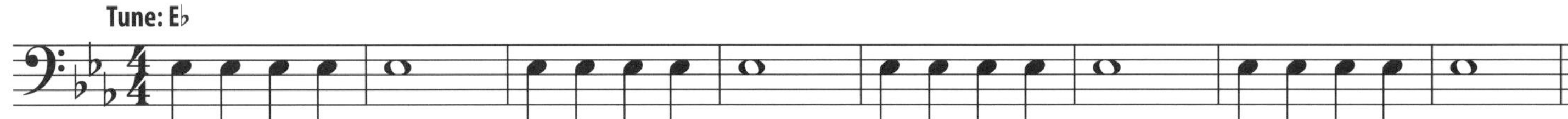

93 **PASSING THE TONIC**

94 **PASSING THE TONIC**

95 **PASSING THE TONIC**

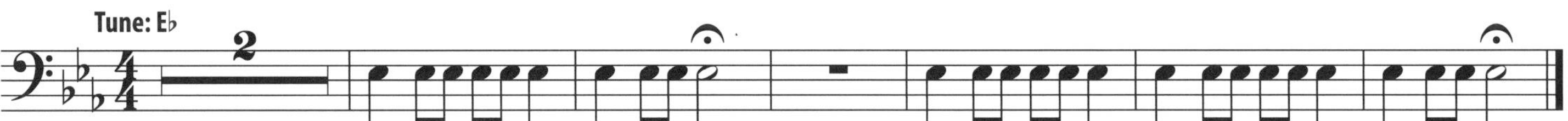

96 **BREATHING AND LONG TONES**

97 **BREATHING AND LONG TONES**

98 **BREATHING AND LONG TONES**

99 **BREATHING AND LONG TONES**

100 CONCERT E♭ MAJOR SCALE

Tune: B♭, E♭

101 SCALE PATTERN

Tune: B♭, E♭

102 SCALE PATTERN

Tune: E♭

103 SCALE PATTERN

Tune: B♭, E♭

104 SCALE PATTERN

Tune: B♭, E♭

105 SCALE PATTERN

Tune: B♭, E♭

106 CHANGING SCALE RHYTHM

Tune: E♭

107 CONCERT E♭ CHROMATIC SCALE

Tune: B♭, E♭

108 FLEXIBILITY

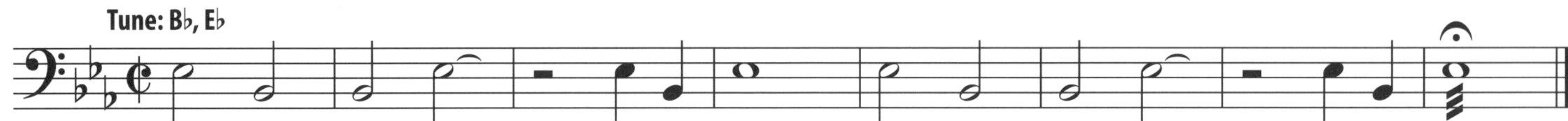

109 FLEXIBILITY

110 ARPEGGIOS

111 ARPEGGIOS

112 INTERVALS

113 INTERVALS

114 BALANCE AND INTONATION: PERFECT INTERVALS

115 BALANCE AND INTONATION: DIATONIC HARMONY

116 BALANCE AND INTONATION: FAMILY BALANCE

117 **BALANCE AND INTONATION: LAYERED TUNING**

118 **BALANCE AND INTONATION: LAYERED TUNING**

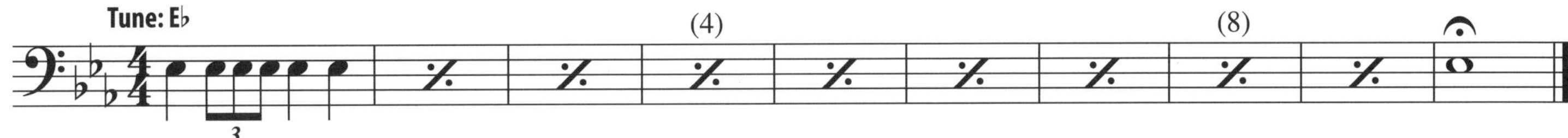

119 **BALANCE AND INTONATION: SHIFTING CHORD QUALITIES**

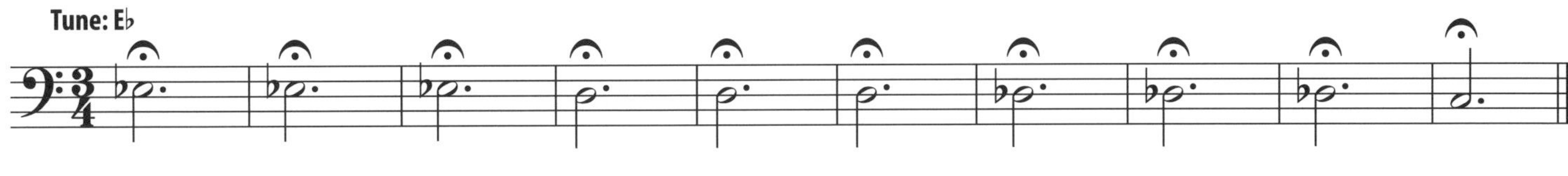

120 **EXPANDING INTERVALS: DOWNWARD IN PARALLEL OCTAVES**

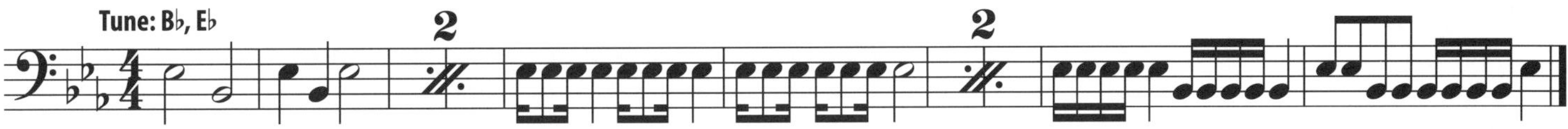

121 **EXPANDING INTERVALS: DOWNWARD IN PARALLEL FIFTHS**

122 **EXPANDING INTERVALS: DOWNWARD IN TRIADS**

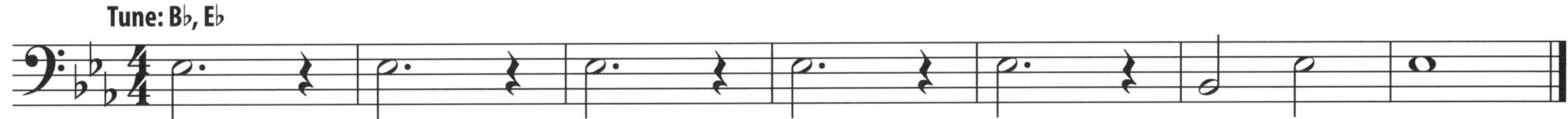

123 **EXPANDING INTERVALS: UPWARD IN PARALLEL OCTAVES**

124 **EXPANDING INTERVALS: UPWARD IN TRIADS**

125 RHYTHM

Tune: E♭

126 RHYTHM

Tune: E♭

127 RHYTHM

Tune: E♭

128 RHYTHM

Tune: E♭

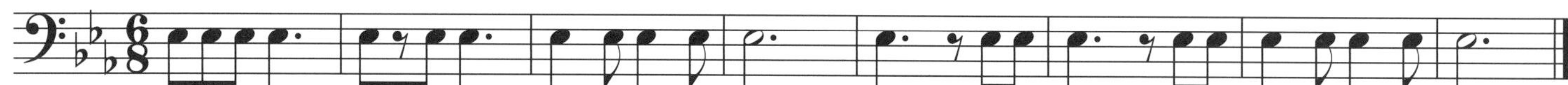

129 RHYTHM

Tune: B♭, E♭, F

130 RHYTHMIC SUBDIVISION

Tune: E♭

131 RHYTHMIC SUBDIVISION

Tune: E♭

132 RHYTHMIC SUBDIVISION

Tune: B♭, E♭

133 METER

134 PHRASING

135 PHRASING

136 ARTICULATION

137 DYNAMICS

138 ETUDE

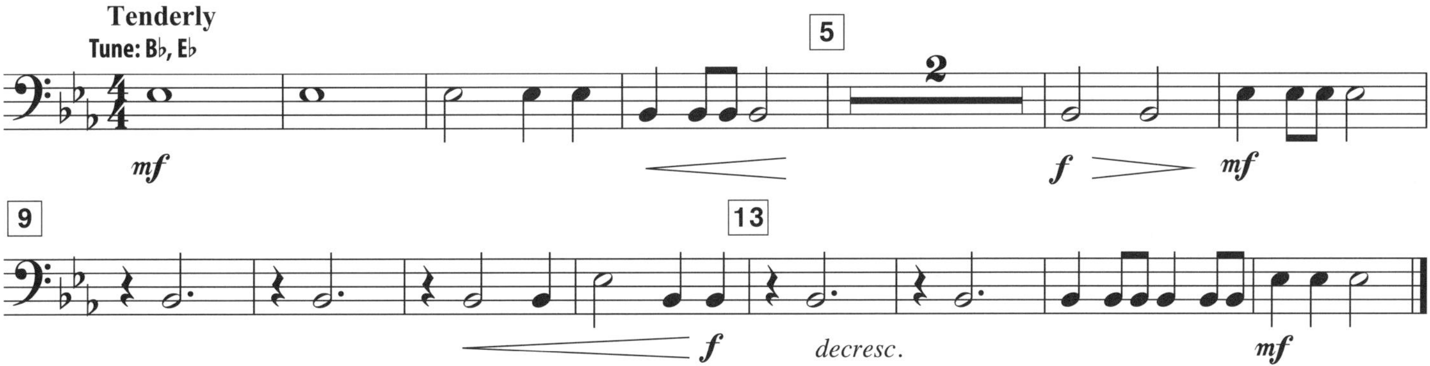

139 ETUDE

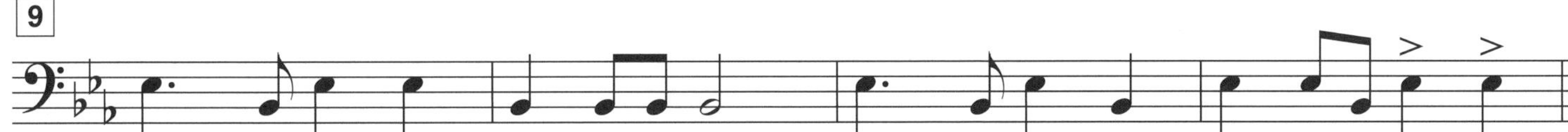

140 **CHORALE**

141 **CHORALE**

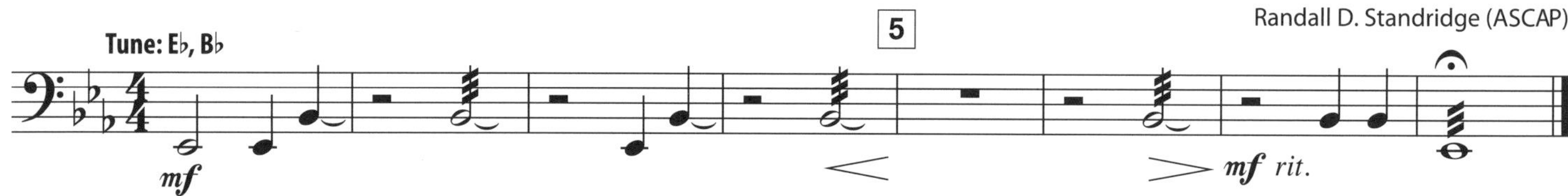

142 **CONCERT E♭ MAJOR SCALE & CHORALE**

143 **CHORALE**

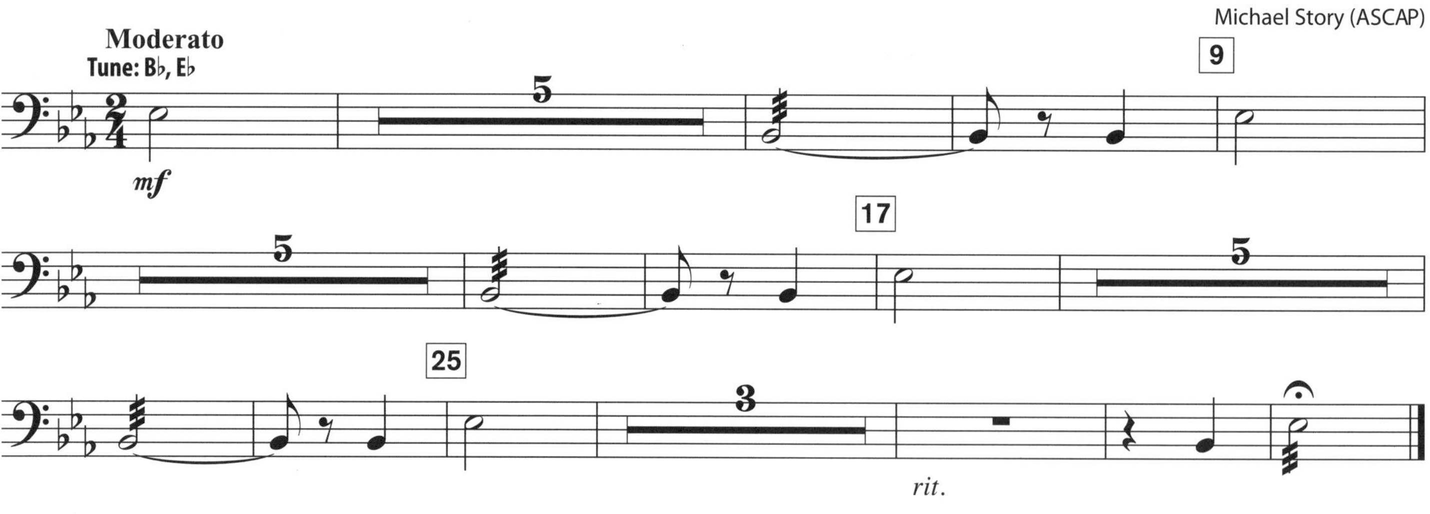

144 **CHORALE**

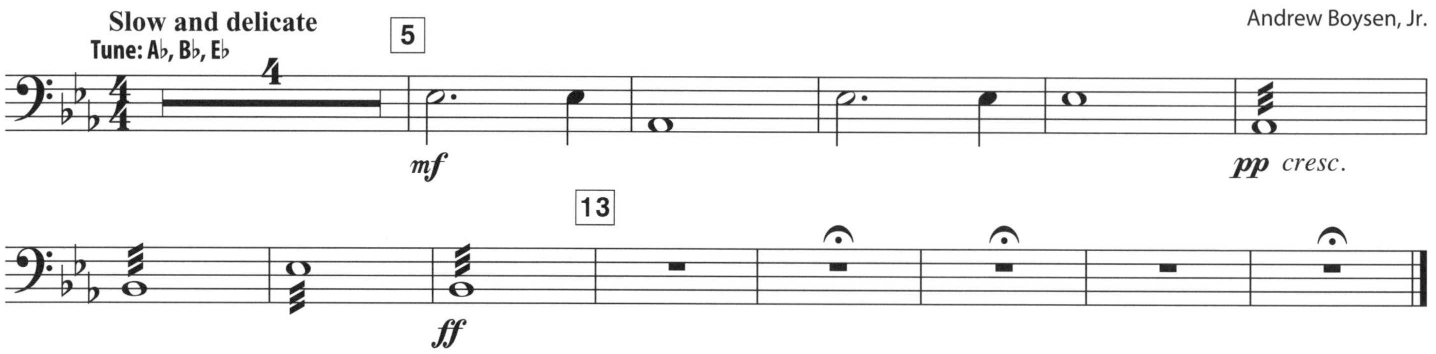

145 CHORALE

146 CHORALE

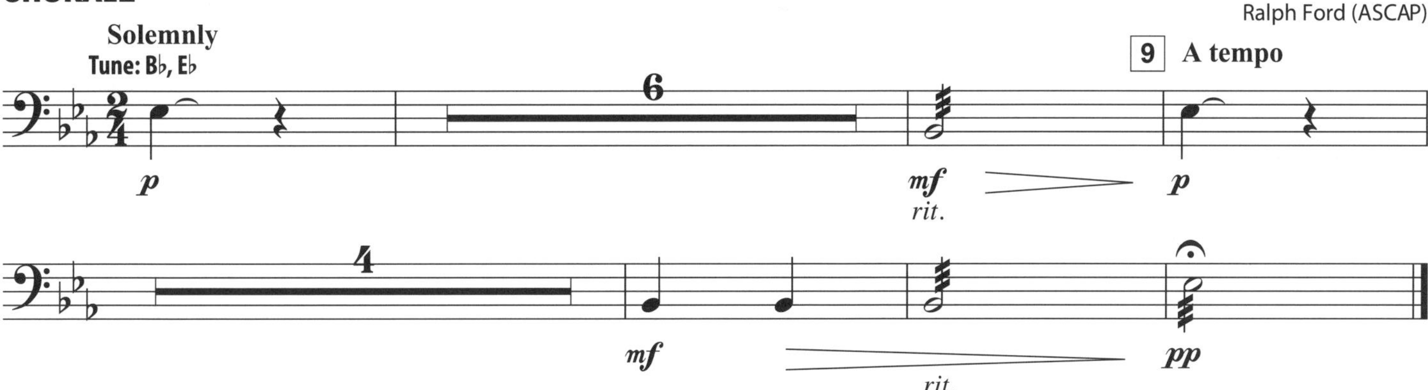

147 CHORALE

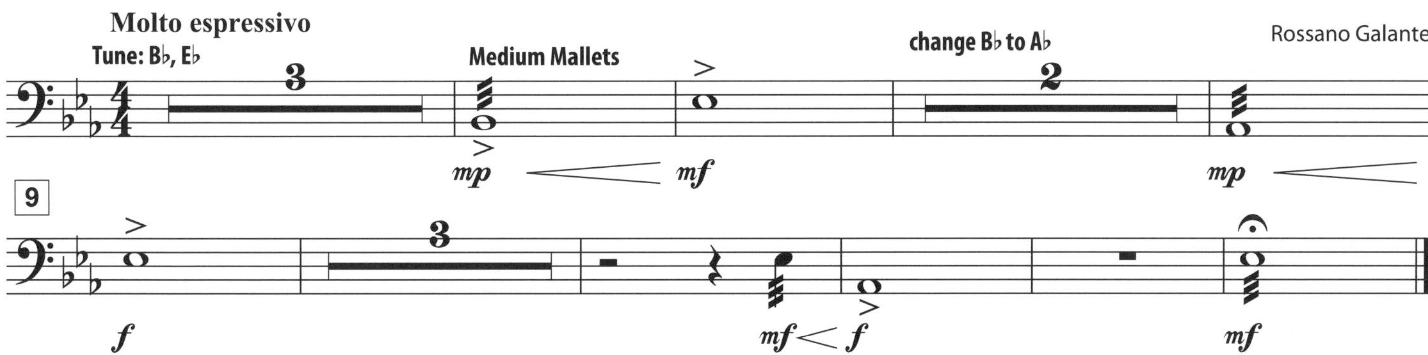

148 CHORALE

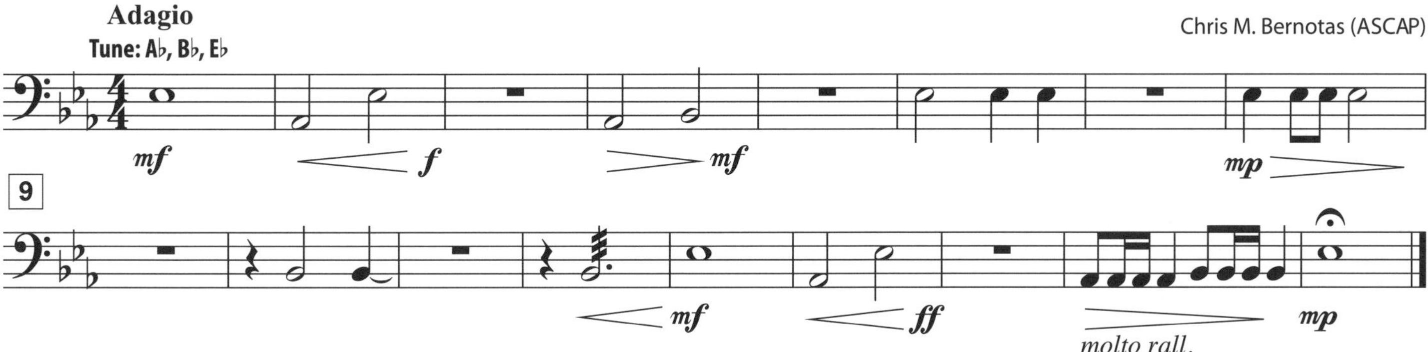

149 CHORALE

Concert C Minor

150 **PASSING THE TONIC**

151 **BREATHING AND LONG TONES**

152 **CONCERT C NATURAL MINOR SCALE**

153 **CONCERT C HARMONIC AND MELODIC MINOR SCALES**

154 **SCALE PATTERN**

155 **CONCERT C CHROMATIC SCALE**

156 **FLEXIBILITY**

157 **FLEXIBILITY**

158 **ARPEGGIOS**

159 **ARPEGGIOS**

160 **INTERVALS**

161 **INTERVALS**

162 **BALANCE AND INTONATION: DIATONIC HARMONY**

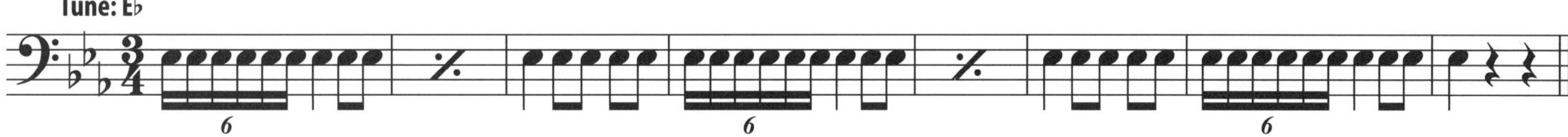

163 **BALANCE AND INTONATION: MOVING CHORD TONES**

164 **BALANCE AND INTONATION: LAYERED TUNING**

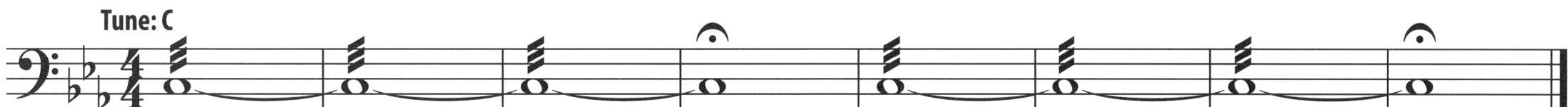

165 **BALANCE AND INTONATION: FAMILY BALANCE**

166 **EXPANDING INTERVALS: DOWNWARD IN TRIADS**

167 **EXPANDING INTERVALS: UPWARD IN TRIADS**

168 RHYTHM

169 RHYTHM

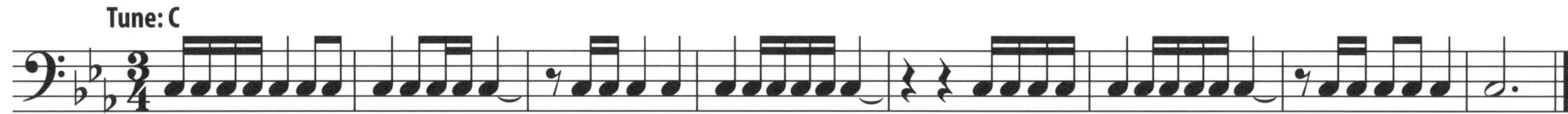

170 RHYTHM

171 RHYTHMIC SUBDIVISION

172 RHYTHMIC SUBDIVISION

173 ARTICULATION AND DYNAMICS

174 ETUDE

175 CHORALE
Randall D. Standridge (ASCAP)
Tune: G, C
5
2
mp
f
rit.
mp
176 CHORALE
Roland Barrett
Tune: G, C, E♭
5
p
mp
p
mf
p
177 CONCERT C MINOR SCALE & CHORALE
Chris M. Bernotas (ASCAP)
A
B
Tune: G, C
mp
178 CHORALE: MEINES LEBENS LETZTE ZEIT
From the Gotha Psalter, 1726
Harmonized by J.S. Bach (1685–1750)
Arranged by Todd Stalter
Maestoso
Tune: G, C, E♭
2
9
mp
17
24
4
179 CHORALE
Rossano Galante
Dark and moody
Tune: F, G, C
5
3
mp
9
13
f
mp
f
mp
f
sfp
ff

Concert F Major

180 **PASSING THE TONIC**

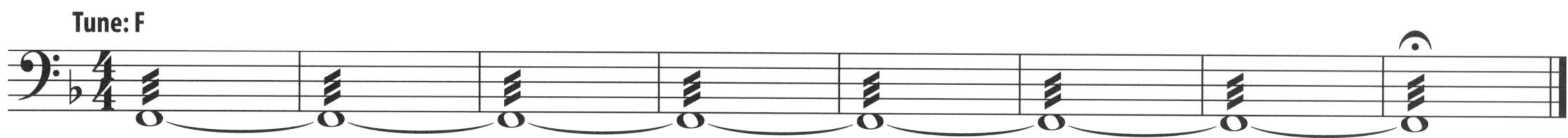

181 **BREATHING AND LONG TONES**

182 **CONCERT F MAJOR SCALE**

183 **SCALE PATTERN**

184 **SCALE PATTERN**

185 **CONCERT F CHROMATIC SCALE**

186 **FLEXIBILITY**

187 **FLEXIBILITY**

188 **ARPEGGIOS**

189 **ARPEGGIOS**

190 **INTERVALS**

191 **BALANCE AND INTONATION: DIATONIC HARMONY**

192 **BALANCE AND INTONATION: FAMILY BALANCE**

193 **BALANCE AND INTONATION: LAYERED TUNING**

194 **BALANCE AND INTONATION: MOVING CHORD TONES**

195 **BALANCE AND INTONATION: SHIFTING CHORD QUALITIES**

196 **EXPANDING INTERVALS: DOWNWARD IN PARALLEL FIFTHS**

197 **EXPANDING INTERVALS: UPWARD IN PARALLEL FIFTHS**

198 **RHYTHM**

199 **RHYTHM**

Tune: F

200 **RHYTHM**

Tune: F

201 **RHYTHMIC SUBDIVISION**

Tune: F, C

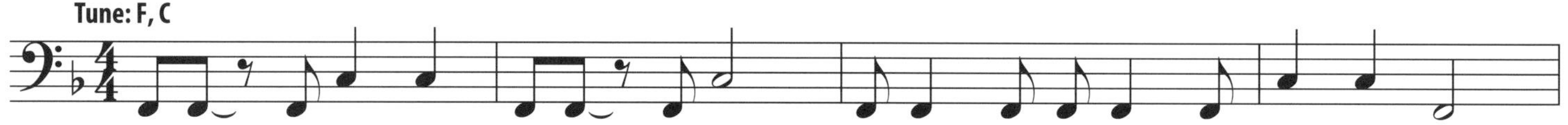

202 **RHYTHMIC SUBDIVISION**

Tune: F

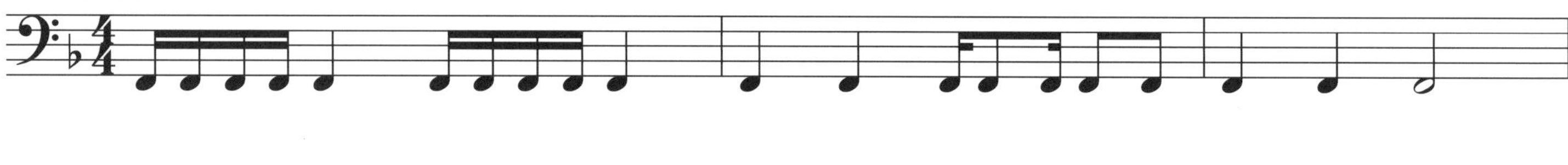

203 **ARTICULATION AND DYNAMICS**

Tune: F, C

204 **ETUDE**

Moderately

Tune: F, C

205 CHORALE: OVERTURE 1812
Pyotr Ilyich Tchaikovsky
Arranged by Michael Story (ASCAP)
Slowly and connected
Tune: C, F
mf
4
rit.
206 CHORALE
Randall D. Standridge (ASCAP)
Tune: F, C
mp
2
2
f
9
rit.
mp
207 CONCERT F MAJOR SCALE & CHORALE
Chris M. Bernotas (ASCAP)
A
B
Tune: F, C
mf
208 CHORALE
Flowing and lyrical
Rossano Galante
Tune: C, D
7
Medium Mallets
9
pp
f
5
mf
p
17
change C to F
6
p
209 CHORALE
Reflective
Ralph Ford (ASCAP)
Tune: F, C
ppp
p
2
p
9
5
mp
p
pp

Concert D Minor

210 PASSING THE TONIC

211 BREATHING AND LONG TONES

212 CONCERT D NATURAL MINOR SCALE

213 CONCERT D HARMONIC AND MELODIC MINOR SCALES

214 SCALE PATTERN

215 SCALE PATTERN

216 CONCERT D CHROMATIC SCALE

217 FLEXIBILITY

218 **FLEXIBILITY**

219 **ARPEGGIOS**

220 **ARPEGGIOS**

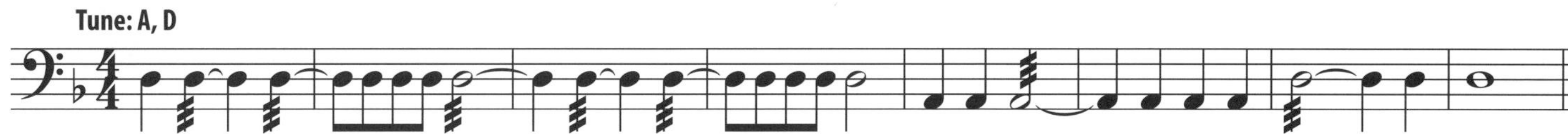

221 **INTERVALS**

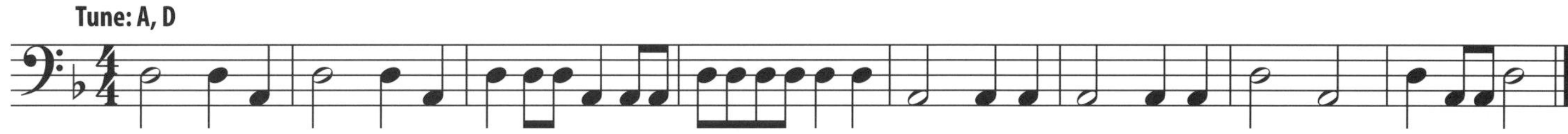

222 **BALANCE AND INTONATION: DIATONIC HARMONY**

223 **BALANCE AND INTONATION: FAMILY BALANCE**

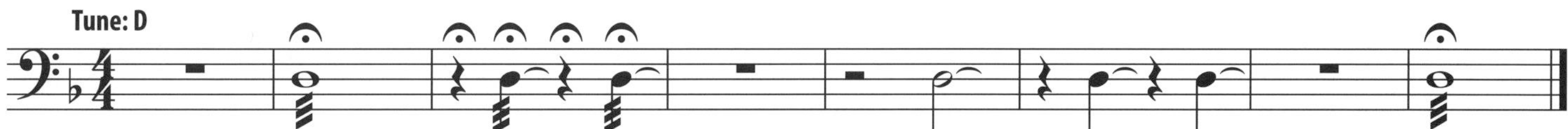

224 **BALANCE AND INTONATION: LAYERED TUNING**

225 **BALANCE AND INTONATON: MOVING CHORD TONES**

226 **EXPANDING INTERVALS: DOWNWARD IN TRIADS**

227 **EXPANDING INTERVALS: UPWARD IN TRIADS**

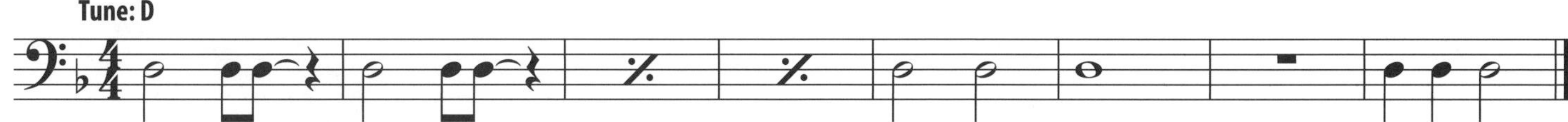

228 **RHYTHM**

229 **RHYTHM**

230 **RHYTHM**

231 **RHYTHMIC SUBDIVISION**

232 **RHYTHMIC SUBDIVISION**

233 **ARTICULATION AND DYNAMICS**

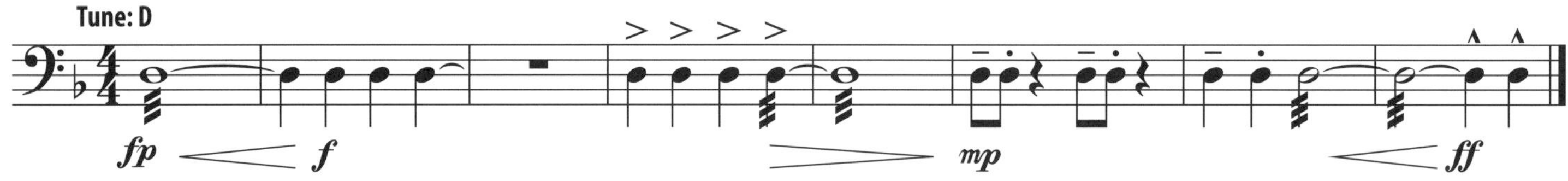

234 **ETUDE**

235 CHORALE
Roland Barrett
Tune: D
p
5
9
13
236 CHORALE
Slow and grave
Andrew Boysen, Jr.
Tune: A, D
2
5
p
f
mf
p
rit.
237 CONCERT D MINOR SCALE & CHORALE
Chris M. Bernotas (ASCAP)
A
B
Tune: A, D
mf
cresc.
f
decresc.
mp
238 CHORALE
Andante
Robert Sheldon
Tune: G, D
3
9
4
mp
f
15
3
2
mp
rall.
mp
239 CHORALE: PSALM 33
From the Genevan Psalter
Harmonized by Claude Goudimel (c. 1520–1572)
Arranged/Edited by Todd Stalter
Grave
Tune: A, D, E
3
mp
8
rit.

Concert A♭ Major

240 **PASSING THE TONIC**

241 **BREATHING AND LONG TONES**

242 **CONCERT A♭ MAJOR SCALE**

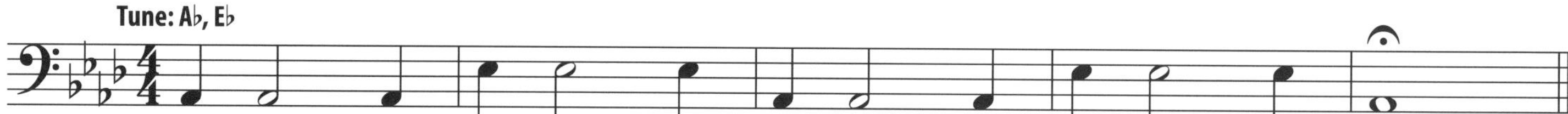

243 **SCALE PATTERN**

244 **SCALE PATTERN**

245 **CONCERT A♭ CHROMATIC SCALE**

246 **FLEXIBILITY**

247 **FLEXIBILITY**

248 **ARPEGGIOS**

249 **ARPEGGIOS**

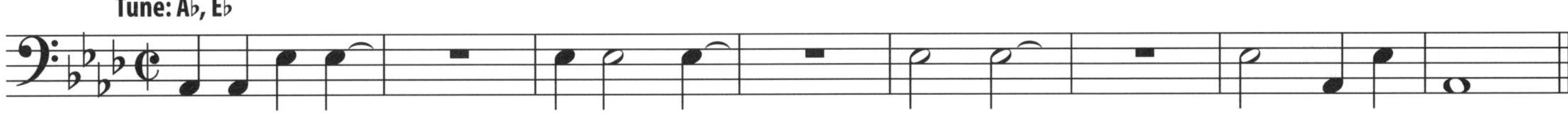

250 **INTERVALS**

251 **BALANCE AND INTONATION: DIATONIC HARMONY**

252 **BALANCE AND INTONATION: FAMILY BALANCE**

253 **BALANCE AND INTONATION: LAYERED TUNING**

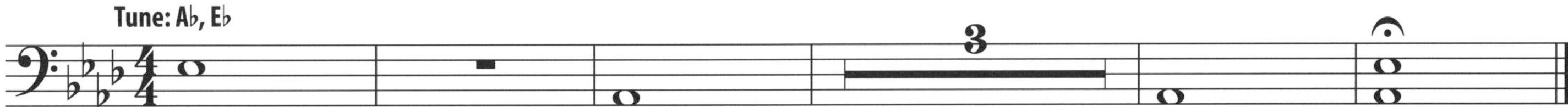

254 **BALANCE AND INTONATION: MOVING CHORD TONES**

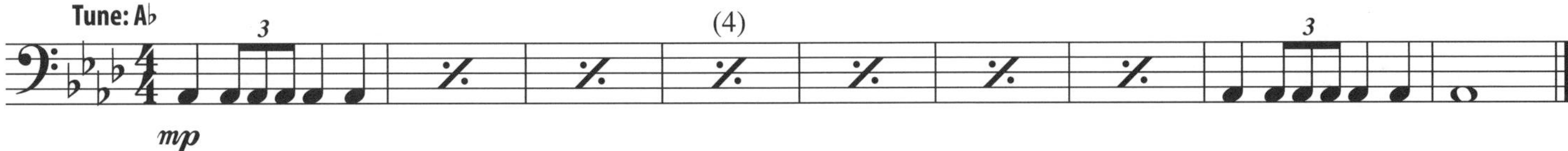

255 **EXPANDING INTERVALS: DOWNWARD IN PARALLEL FIFTHS**

256 **EXPANDING INTERVALS: UPWARD IN PARALLEL THIRDS**

257 RHYTHM

Tune: A♭

258 RHYTHM

Tune: A♭

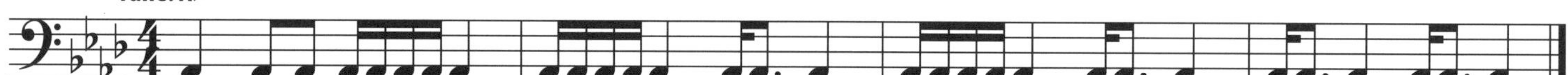

259 RHYTHM

Tune: A♭

260 RHYTHMIC SUBDIVISION

Tune: A♭, E♭

261 RHYTHMIC SUBDIVISION

Tune: A♭, E♭

262 DYNAMICS

Tune: A♭, E♭

263 ARTICULATION AND DYNAMICS

Tune: A♭, E♭

264 ETUDE

Moderately

Tune: A♭, D♭, E♭

265 CHORALE

Randall D. Standridge (ASCAP)

266 CHORALE

Andrew Boysen, Jr.

267 CONCERT A♭ MAJOR SCALE & CHORALE

Chris M. Bernotas (ASCAP)

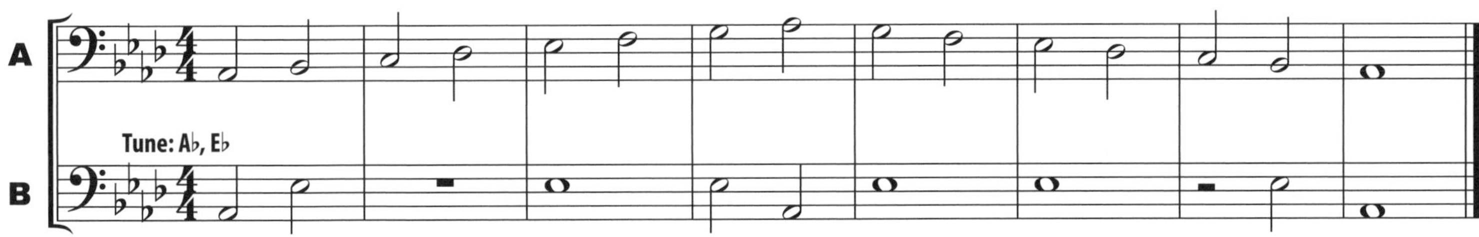

268 CHORALE

Ralph Ford (ASCAP)

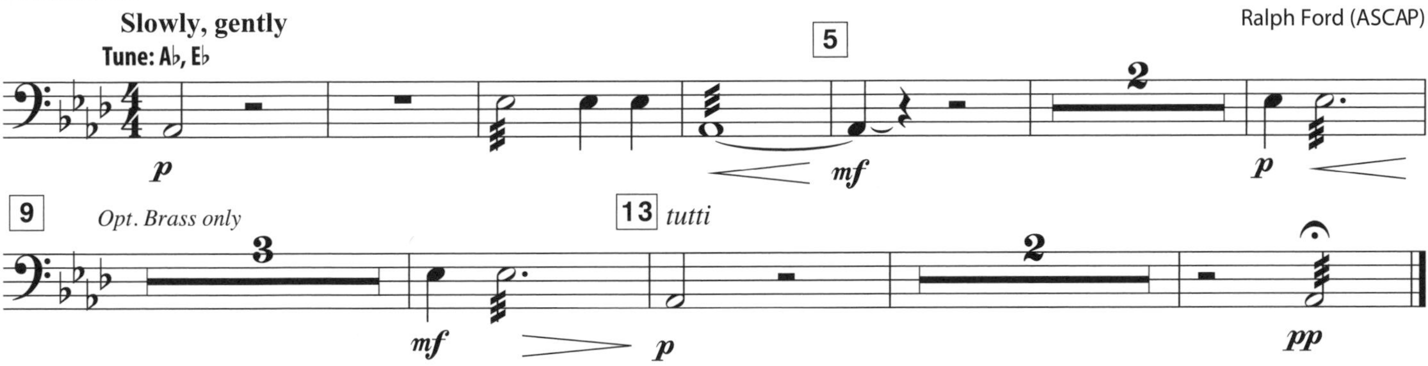

269 CHORALE

Roland Barrett

Concert F Minor

270 PASSING THE TONIC

271 BREATHING AND LONG TONES

272 CONCERT F NATURAL MINOR SCALE

273 CONCERT F HARMONIC AND MELODIC MINOR SCALES

274 SCALE PATTERN

275 CONCERT F CHROMATIC SCALE

276 FLEXIBILITY

277 FLEXIBILITY

278 ARPEGGIOS

279 ARPEGGIOS

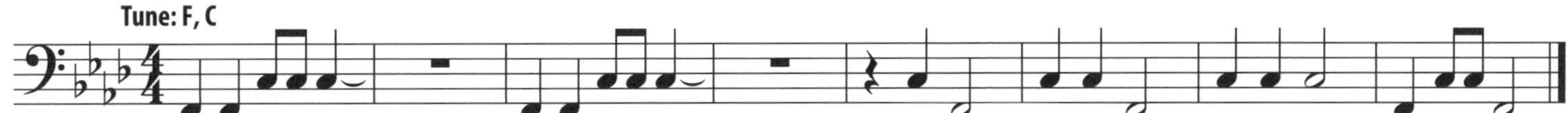

280 INTERVALS

281 INTERVALS

282 BALANCE AND INTONATION: DIATONIC HARMONY

283 BALANCE AND INTONATION: FAMILY BALANCE

284 BALANCE AND INTONATION: LAYERED TUNING

285 BALANCE AND INTONATION: MOVING CHORD TONES

286 EXPANDING INTERVALS: DOWNWARD IN TRIADS

287 EXPANDING INTERVALS: UPWARD IN TRIADS

288 RHYTHM

289 RHYTHM

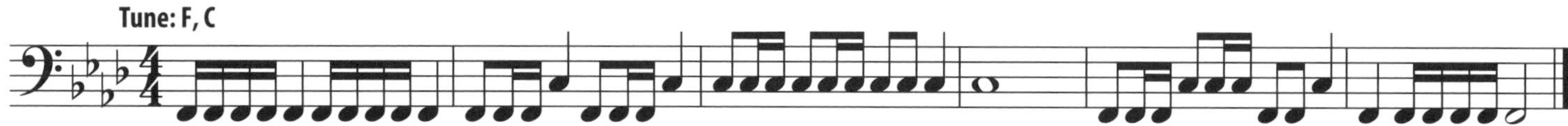

290 RHYTHM

291 RHYTHMIC SUBDIVISION

292 RHYTHMIC SUBDIVISION

293 ARTICULATION AND DYNAMICS

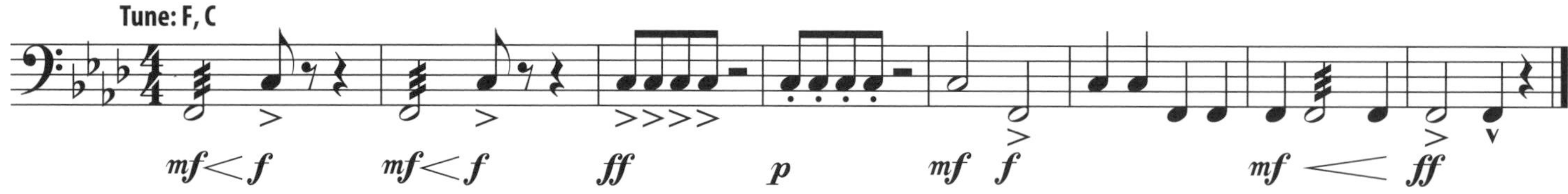

294 ETUDE

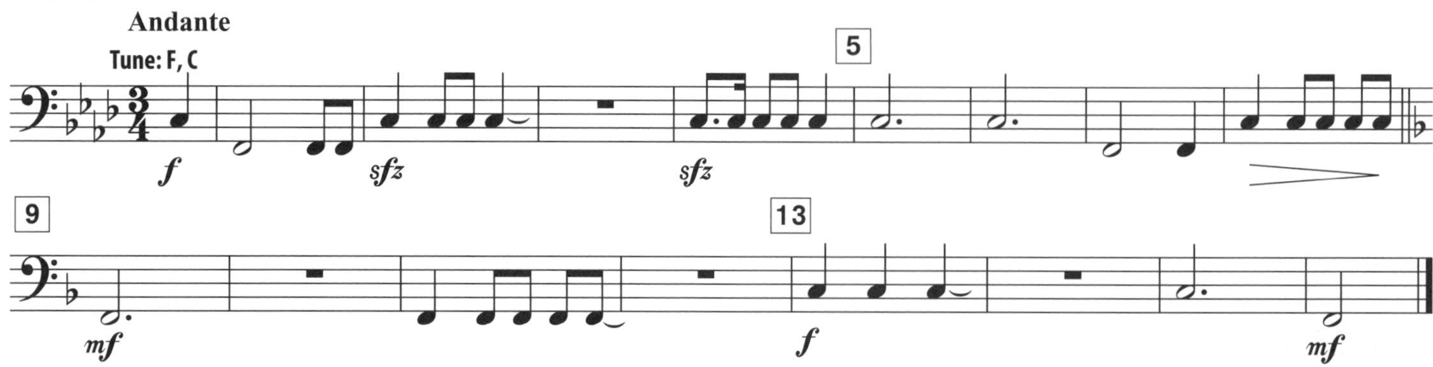

295 **CHORALE**

Randall D. Standridge (ASCAP)

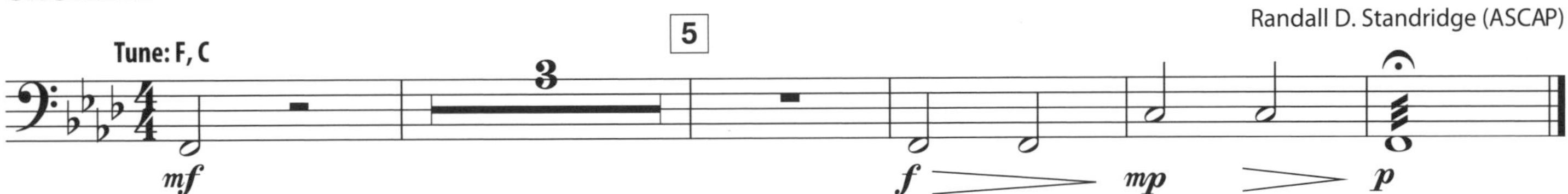

296 **CHORALE**

Roland Barrett

297 **CONCERT F MINOR SCALE & CHORALE**

Chris M. Bernotas (ASCAP)

298 **CHORALE**

Robert Sheldon

299 **CHORALE**

Ralph Ford (ASCAP)

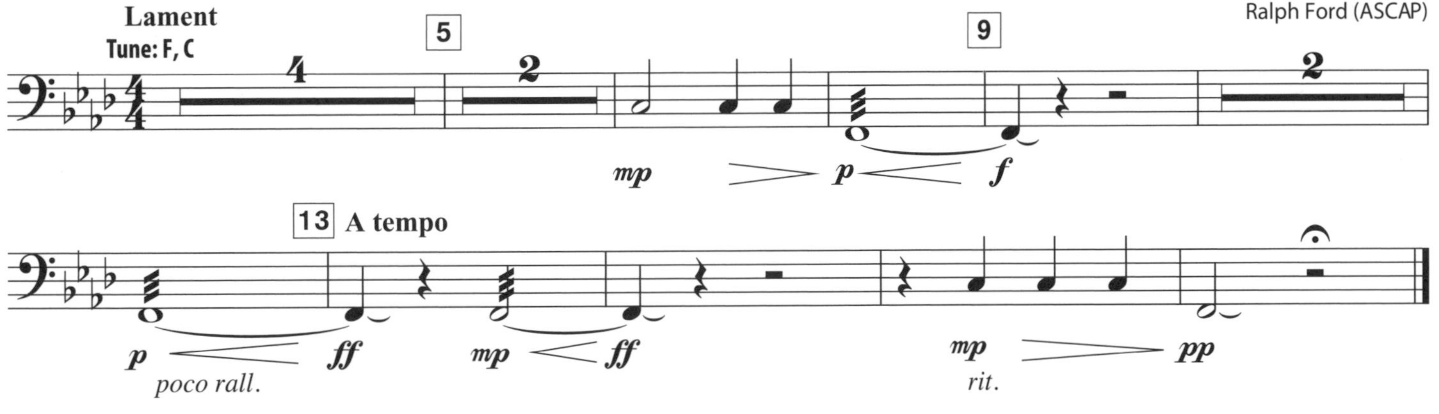

Concert D♭ Major

300 **BREATHING AND LONG TONES**

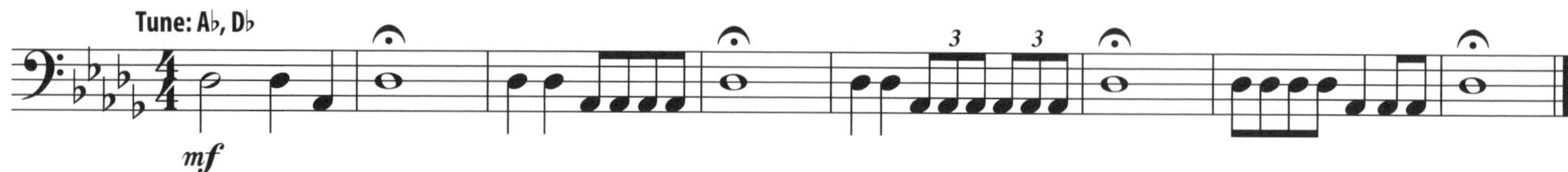

301 **CONCERT D♭ MAJOR SCALE**

302 **SCALE PATTERN**

303 **SCALE PATTERN**

304 **SCALE PATTERN**

305 **FLEXIBILITY**

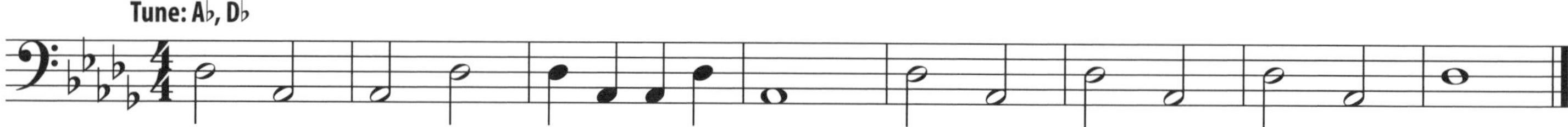

306 **ARPEGGIOS**

307 **INTERVALS**

308 **BALANCE AND INTONATION: FAMILY BALANCE**

309 **BALANCE AND INTONATION: LAYERED TUNING**

310 **EXPANDING INTERVALS: DOWNWARD AND UPWARD IN PARALLEL OCTAVES**

311 **ARTICULATION AND DYNAMICS**

312 **ETUDE**

313 **ETUDE**

314 **CHORALE**

Andrew Boysen, Jr.

315 **CHORALE**

Todd Stalter

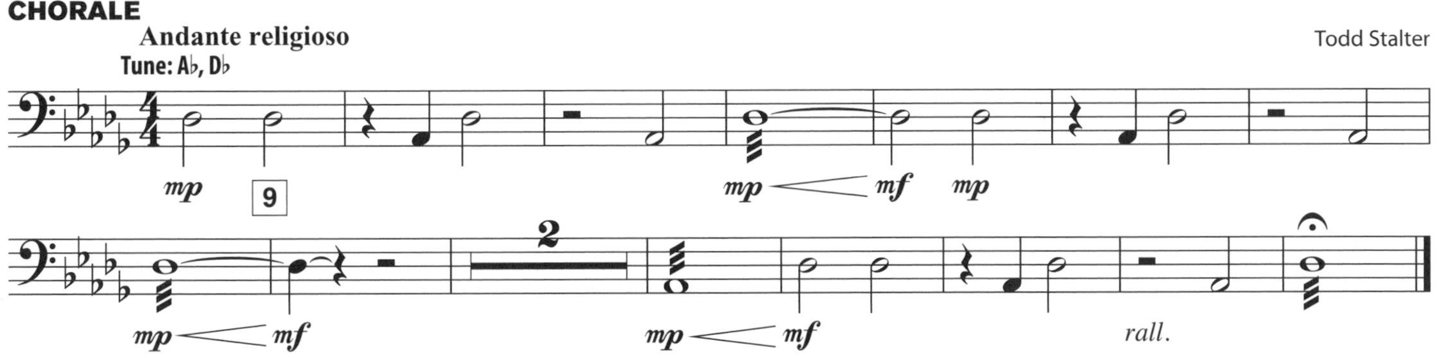

Concert B♭ Minor

316 **BREATHING AND LONG TONES**

317 **CONCERT B♭ NATURAL MINOR SCALE**

318 **CONCERT B♭ HARMONIC AND MELODIC MINOR SCALES**

319 **SCALE PATTERN**

320 **SCALE PATTERN**

321 **FLEXIBILITY**

322 **ARPEGGIOS**

323 **INTERVALS**

324 **BALANCE AND INTONATION: LAYERED TUNING**

325 **BALANCE AND INTONATION: MOVING CHORD TONES**

326 **EXPANDING INTERVALS: DOWNWARD IN TRIADS**

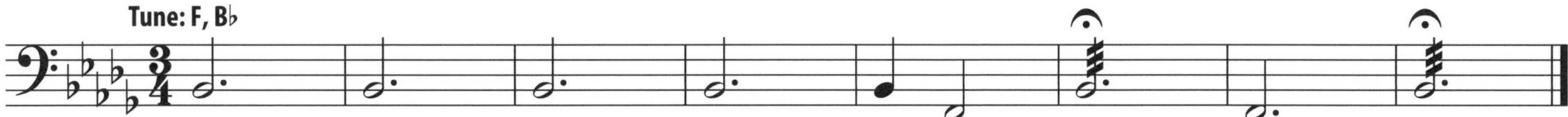

327 **ARTICULATION AND DYNAMICS**

328 **ETUDE**

329 **ETUDE**

330 **CHORALE**

331 **CHORALE**

Concert C Major

332 **BREATHING AND LONG TONES**

Tune: G, C

333 **CONCERT C MAJOR SCALE**

Tune: G, C

334 **SCALE PATTERN**

Tune: G, C

335 **SCALE PATTERN**

Tune: G, C

336 **FLEXIBILITY**

Tune: G, C

337 **ARPEGGIOS**

Tune: G, C

338 **INTERVALS**

Tune: G, C

339 **INTERVALS**

Tune: G, C

340 **BALANCE AND INTONATION: FAMILY BALANCE**

Tune: C

341 **BALANCE AND INTONATION: LAYERED TUNING**

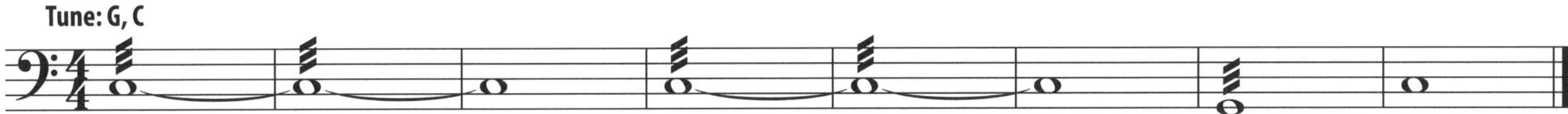

342 **EXPANDING INTERVALS: DOWNWARD IN PARALLEL FIFTHS**

343 **ARTICULATION AND DYNAMICS**

344 **ETUDE**

Stately

345 **ETUDE**

346 **CHORALE**

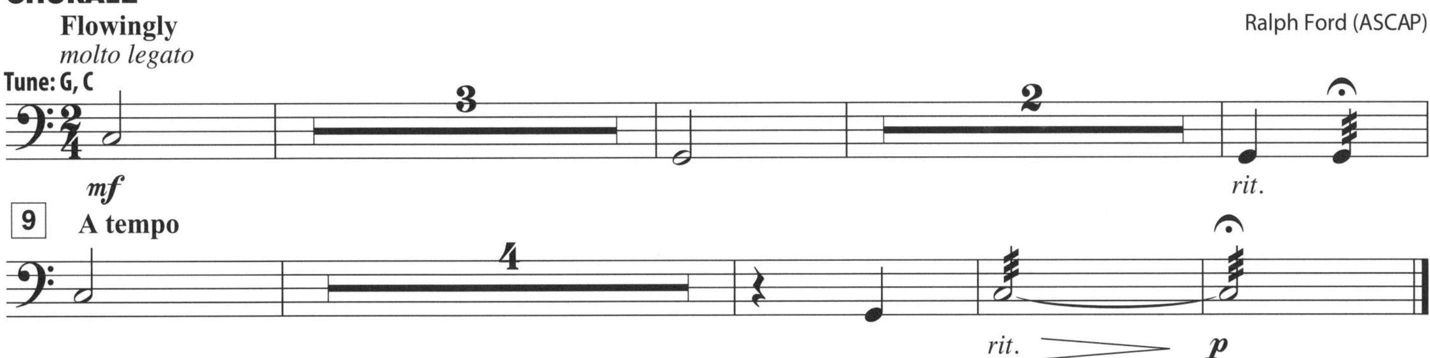

347 **CHORALE: LARGO FROM THE "NEW WORLD SYMPHONY"**

Concert A Minor

348 **BREATHING AND LONG TONES**

349 **CONCERT A NATURAL MINOR SCALE**

350 **CONCERT A HARMONIC AND MELODIC MINOR SCALES**

351 **SCALE PATTERN**

352 **FLEXIBILITY**

353 **ARPEGGIOS**

354 **INTERVALS**

355 **INTERVALS**

356 **BALANCE AND INTONATION: DIATONIC HARMONY**

357 **BALANCE AND INTONATION: FAMILY BALANCE**

358 **EXPANDING INTERVALS: DOWNWARD IN TRIADS**

359 **ARTICULATION AND DYNAMICS**

360 **ETUDE**

361 **ETUDE**

362 **CHORALE**

363 **CHORALE**

Concert G Major

364 **CONCERT G MAJOR SCALE**

365 **BALANCE AND INTONATION: FAMILY BALANCE**

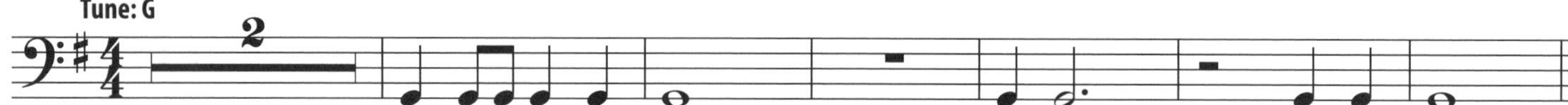

366 **ETUDE**

367 **CHORALE**

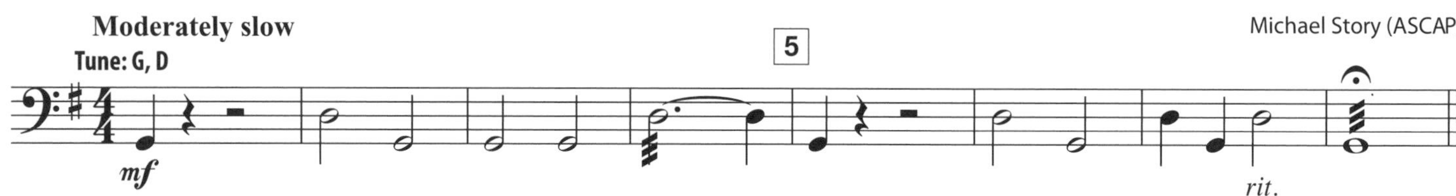

Concert E Minor

368 **CONCERT E NATURAL MINOR SCALE**

369 **CONCERT E HARMONIC AND MELODIC MINOR SCALES**

370 **BALANCE AND INTONATION: LAYERED TUNING**

371 **ETUDE**

372 **CHORALE**

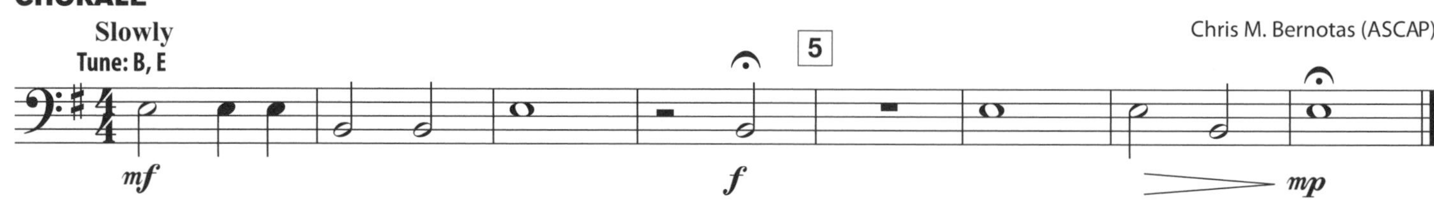

Advancing Rhythm and Meter

383 6/8 METER

Tune: B♭

384 6/8 METER

Tune: B♭

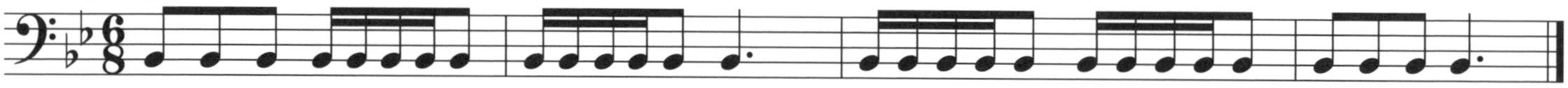

385 6/8 METER

Tune: F, B♭

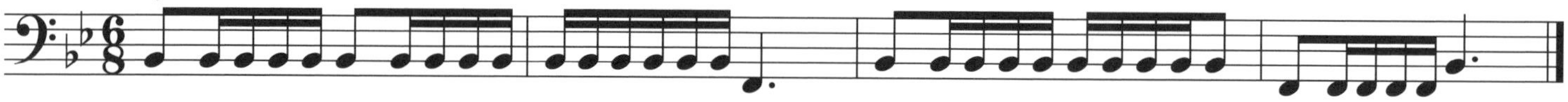

386 6/8 METER

Tune: F, B♭

387 6/8 METER

Tune: B♭

388 6/8 METER

Tune: F, B♭

389 6/8 METER

Tune: F, B♭

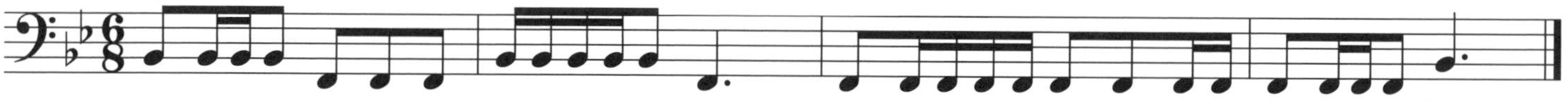

390 6/8 METER

Tune: F, B♭

391 CHANGING METERS: 4/4 AND 6/8

Tune: F, B♭

(♪ = ♪)

392 CHANGING METERS: 3/4 AND 6/8

Tune: F, B♭

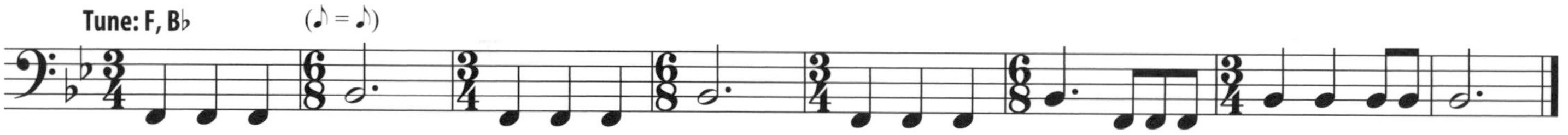

(♪ = ♪)

393 **TRIPLETS**

394 **TRIPLETS**

395 **TRIPLETS**

396 **TRIPLETS**

397 **TRIPLETS**

398 **TRIPLETS**

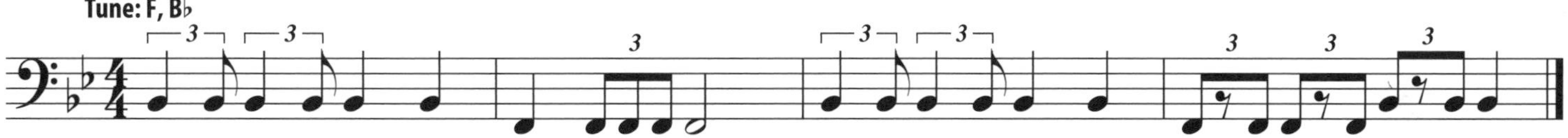

399 **TRIPLETS**

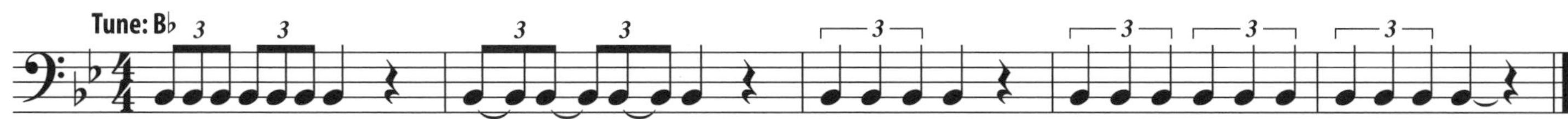

400 **TRIPLETS**

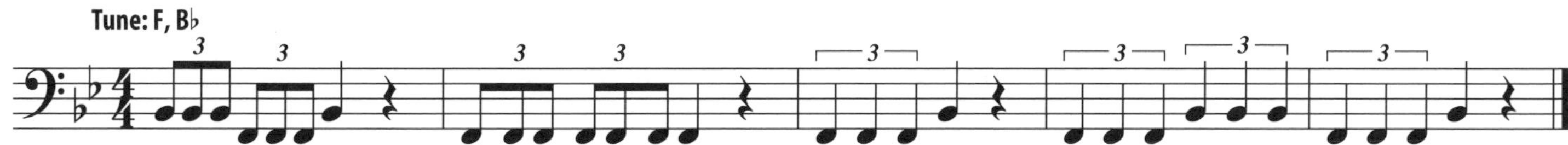

401 **TRIPLETS**

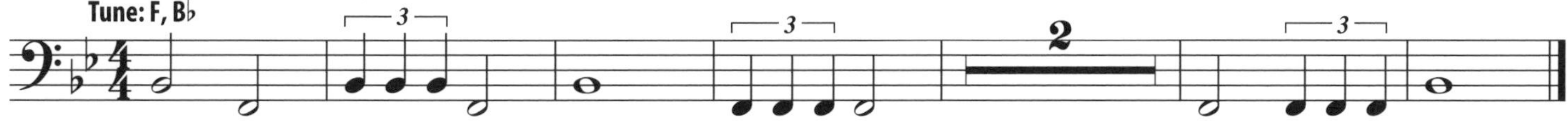

402 **TRIPLETS**

403 $\frac{3}{8}$ **METER**

Tune: B♭

404 $\frac{3}{8}$ **METER**

Tune: F, B♭

405 $\frac{9}{8}$ **METER**

Tune: B♭

406 $\frac{9}{8}$ **METER**

Tune: F, B♭

407 $\frac{12}{8}$ **METER**

Tune: B♭

408 $\frac{12}{8}$ **METER**

Tune: F, B♭

409 $\frac{5}{8}$ **METER**

(2+3)
Tune: B♭
(3+2)

410 $\frac{5}{8}$ **METER**

(2+3)
Tune: F, B♭
(3+2)

411 $\frac{7}{8}$ **METER**

(2+2+3)
Tune: B♭

412 $\frac{7}{8}$ **METER**

(2+2+3)
Tune: F, B♭

Timpani

THE PARTS OF THE TIMPANI

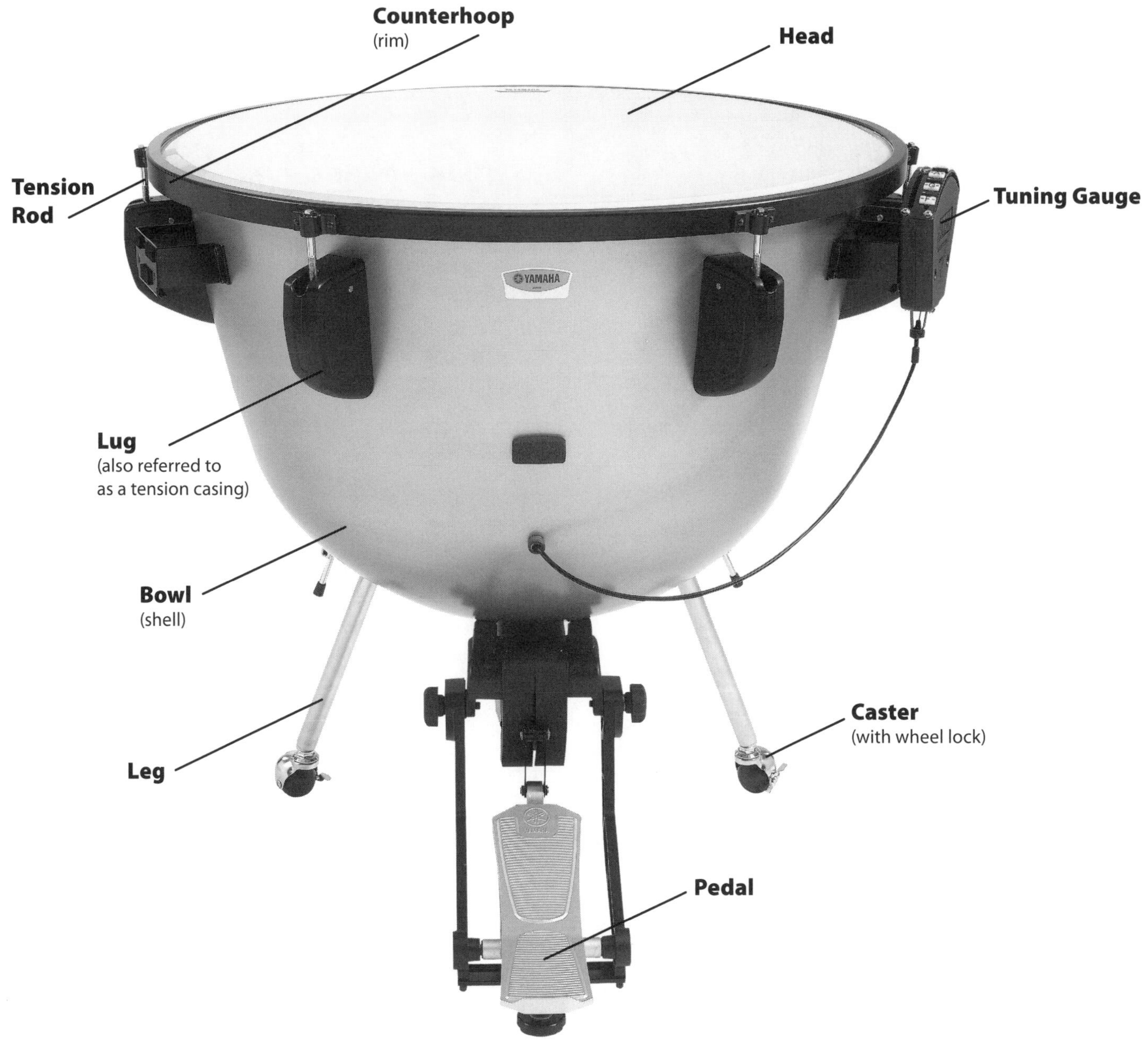

TIMPANI RANGES

With the pedals down to their lowest position, set the proper range of each drum by tuning the head to the following fundamental notes. When using only two drums, it is recommended you use the 26- and 29-inch drums.

32" = D	26" = B♭
29" = F	23" = D

INSTRUMENT PLACEMENT & PLAYING POSITION

Timpani are usually positioned so the lowest drum is to your left. If using more than two drums, arrange them in a semi-circle with the pedals facing you.

Stand behind the drums with your feet comfortably spread for proper balance and weight distribution. Some players prefer to lean against a stool to help facilitate pedal changes and to bring the arm position down to a comfortable playing position.

THE MALLET GRIP

The "German" grip, as opposed to the "French" grip, is often used by beginning players and is similar to the matched grip used for playing the snare drum. Let's review the matched grip:

A. First, extend your right hand as if you were going to shake hands with someone.

B. Place the mallet between your thumb and the first joint of your index finger, approximately 1/3 the way up from the end of the mallet.

C. Curve the other fingers around the shaft of the mallet.

D. Turn your hand over so your palm is facing towards the floor.

E. Repeat steps A–D with your left hand.

TUNING

Most beginning students start off matching the pitch from an external source such as a pitch pipe or keyboard percussion instrument. It is important to listen for pitch relationships within the ensemble (soloist, chord, etc.) and to check your tuning periodically.

STRIKING THE DRUM

Depending on the size of the drum, strike the head about 2 to 5 inches in from the bowl's edge making sure the heads of both mallets are side by side (refer to the diagram on page 28). To produce the best tone, the forearms should be relaxed and nearly parallel to the floor when the head is struck. Immediately following impact, the mallet should rebound without restriction.

ROLLS

The timpani roll is one of the most characteristic sounds of the instrument and is produced by using rapidly alternating single strokes. Rolls are notated in the same manner as those for snare drum.

MUFFLING/DAMPENING

In order to control the amount of sustain, it may be necessary to dampen/muffle the head. This can be accomplished by using the last two or three fingers of either hand to stop the vibration. Players will sometimes dampen a note simultaneously while striking another to avoid the mixture of the two sounds.

CARE & MAINTENANCE

When not in use, heads should be covered with fiberboard discs and mallets should be kept in a stick bag or case. When moving the instrument, lift the drum from the struts rather than the counterhoop. When rolling or moving the drums over a threshold, make sure you lift the pedal mechanism from the floor.